THE SINK for KIDS!

LEAVE IT BETTER

BY WALTER NUSBAUM
AND DAREN MARTIN, PHD

The SINK for KIDS!: Leave it Better

Published by Clovercroft Publishing, Franklin, Tennessee

Cover and Interior Design by Will von Bolton

Printed in the United States of America

ISBN 978-1-956370-87-4

Sometimes the **BEST LESSONS** are **UNEXPECTED**

When Dominic started first grade, he had an experience that would change his life forever.

Not just his life would be changed that day, but the lives of everyone that he would meet.

Walking into the school bathroom, Dominic noticed Grayson, a Third Grader, wiping down the sink.

Grayson was Dominic's neighbor, and he looked up to the older boy. "Isn't that the custodian's job?" Dominic asked. Grayson smiled and said the words that changed Dominic's life forever ...

"Why not leave it better than you found it?"

Dominic was surprised by Grayson's response!

As he thought about it throughout the day, it began to make sense.

"Grayson is so right!" Dominic realized.

If everyone just did their part, the whole school would be better for everyone.

The next time Dominic used the bathroom, something was different. He found himself wiping down the sink after drying his hands. Grayson's words were sinking in

"Why not leave it better?"

Dominic began to "leave it better" every time he used a bathroom.

Not just once ... but every time.

And not just at school ...
... **but everywhere**

Leave it better.

"Wow," he thought, "This little idea can make a BIG difference."

What if we did this ALL the time?

What would it look like if we ALL left things better as a way of life?

Our schools, communities, relationships, and world would ALL be better.

But where would I start?

Maybe I could start by...

- **Leaving myself better**
- **Leaving others better**
- **Leaving the world better**

Leaving myself better might include ...

- **Eating healthy and getting a good night's sleep**
- **Trying my best to learn new things**
- **Staying calm when things don't go my way**
- **Being kind to myself**

What other ways can YOU leave YOURSELF BETTER?

Leaving others better might look like ...

- Being kind to others
- Smiling at people
- Saying "thank you"
- Giving someone a compliment

What other ways can YOU leave OTHERS BETTER?

Leaving the WORLD better includes ...

- **My HOME**
- **My SCHOOL**
- **My COMMUNITY**

Leaving things better at home might look like ...

- **Cooperating with parents and siblings**
- **Cleaning my room**
- **Helping with the dishes**
- **Helping put away groceries**

Leaving things better at school might look like ...

- Bringing a positive attitude to school every day
- Encouraging my classmates and teacher
- Cleaning up trash on the playground
- Paying attention when others are speaking

What other ways can YOU leave THINGS BETTER AT SCHOOL?

Leaving things better in your community might look like ...

- Cleaning up trash
- Helping an elderly neighbor with yard work
- Recycling
- Bringing in carts from the parking lot at the grocery store

What other ways can YOU leave THINGS BETTER IN YOUR COMMUNITY?

Here's an easy way to remember how to

LIVE the SINK Principle:

SEE the need
INVEST yourself
NO act is too small
KEEP it going

SEE THE NEED

STOP RIGHT NOW.
Look around.

What do you see?

There are possibilities everywhere to make the world a better place.

Look for ways **YOU**
can leave things better for
EVERYONE !

INVEST YOURSELF

Many people wait for someone else to take care of things.

It's easy to say ...

- It's not my job
- Someone else will take care of it
- I'll do it later

These attitudes do NOT lead to greatness. Great people invest time and energy to leave it better.

Be great today! Invest yourself!

NO ACT IS TOO SMALL

Do you ever wonder what difference YOU can make?

Everything matters. Small actions can achieve BIG results.

When you see an opportunity to leave it better, take action!

It all starts with YOU!

KEEP IT GOING

The SINK principle is a way of life to be shared. You don't just teach it; you have to demonstrate it to inspire others to do the same things.

If Grayson had just TOLD Dominic about the importance of leaving things better, it would have been just talk.

By leading through his example, Grayson inspired Dominic to take action.

Lead through YOUR action!

After living the SINK principle, Dominic realized something very interesting:

It feels GREAT to leave things better.

Others began to follow Dominic's example !

Mason and Bryce saw what was happening and started living the SINK principle on the playground by looking for kids to include in their games.

4th Graders Caden and Diego noticed what they were doing and mentioned it in class, inspiring a group of girls to start a playground clean-up project.

Brooke and Kianna told some 5th graders, and more and more kids started to get involved with ways to improve the school.

Throughout the year, the whole school began to use the SINK principle to make Sereno Elementary a better place for all.

What would the world look like if we all left things better?

There's only one way to find out ...

GO FIND YOUR
SINK!

One person CAN make a difference in the world. In fact, it is always because of one person that all changes that matter in the world came about. SO BE THAT ONE PERSON!

- BUCKMINSTER FULLER

Just one spark can set the world on fire, so let's get after it and set the world ablaze one SINK at a time!

Invest in your children and their friends today. Contact us about bulk pricing to instill **the SINK principle** in your kids' school, church, sports team, organization and more.

info@TheSinkPrinciple.com

MY SINK COMMITMENT:

I, ________________________________,

commit every day to leave myself, others, and the world better!

Signature ______________________

Date ______________________

Make the commitment today.

A message to YOU from Walter and Daren

We hope you enjoyed our book.

We are so proud of you.

You are a difference-maker!

Please write to us and share how YOU are making YOUR world a better place!

Info@TheSinkPrinciple.com

We can't wait to hear how you leave things better.

WALTER NUSBAUM

Author, Speaker, and Transformation Expert

Walter Nusbaum has spoken to and worked closely with thousands of leaders from all over the world. His core message is that effective transformations require the right actions at the right time.
This is where extraordinary success is found. Connect with him at TheNusbaumGroup.com or Walter@TheNusbaumGroup.com.

DAREN MARTIN, PHD

The Culture Architect, Global Speaker, WSJ & USA Today Bestselling Author

Daren does transformational work with leaders from a wide range of industries all over the world. He is an in-demand keynote speaker who fully engages crowds with action inducing content. His other books include, A Company of Owners, Whiteboard, and many more. Connect with him at DarenMartin.com or Daren@DarenMartin.com

A BIG thanks to Dan Casetta for contributions to the The Sink for Kids!

You can connect with Dan at DanCasetta.com or DanCasetta@gmail.com